Prayers from Prison

A Biblical Study of Faith in Captivity

Brenda S. Jackson, PhD

*Priority*ONE
publications
Detroit, Michigan USA

Prayers from Prison:
A Biblical Study of Faith in Captivity
Copyright © 2019 Brenda S. Jackson, PhD

All Scripture quotations, unless otherwise indicated, are taken from the Holy Bible, New International Version®, NIV®. Copyright ©1973, 1978, 1984, 2011 by Biblica, Inc.™ Used by permission of Zondervan. All rights reserved worldwide. www.zondervan.com The "NIV" and "New International Version" are trademarks registered in the United States Patent and Trademark Office by Biblica, Inc.™

All rights reserved. No part of this publication may be reproduced, stored in a retrieval system, or transmitted in any form or by any means – electronic, mechanical, photocopy, recording, or any other – except for brief quotations in printed reviews, without the prior permission of the publisher.

*Priority*ONE Publications
P. O. Box 361332 | Grosse Pointe, MI48236
E-mail: info@priorityonebooks.com
URL: http://www.priorityonebooks.com

ISBN 13:   978-1-933972-65-7
ISBN 10:   1-933972-65-3

Editing by Patricia Hicks
Cover and Interior design by Christina Dixon

Printed in the United States of America

TABLE OF CONTENTS

INTRODUCTION 5
    PRISONS AND PRAYERS
    What are Biblical prisons?
    What Prayer Is
    The Godhead and Prayer is Key to the Prayer Process:

Prisoner #1 11
    Sampson – Judges 16:28-30
    SIN AND PRAYER

Prisoner #2 13
    Jeremiah's Conversation with God: Jeremiah 6:10
    HELP

Prisoner #3 15
    Jonah, A prophet in a living prison: Jonah 2:2-9
    My Personal Prison

Prisoner #4 19
    Rich man, a sinner sentenced to eternal imprisonment:
    Luke 16:22-24; 26-28
    Prayer and Repentance

Prisoner #5 23
    The Prayers of Apostle Paul during His Imprisonments

    Prayer from a Dungeon: Acts 16:25-34

    Free in a Cage

Pauline Epistle in Prison: Ephesians 1:15-20

Thanksgiving

A Prayer for The Ephesians: Ephesians 3:14-21

The Bond that Binds Family

Paul's Prayer for Philippians: Philippians 1:1-11

Prisoner's Love

Knowing God's Will: Colossians 1:9-14

Not My Will But Your Will

Prisoner #6 35

    The Imprisoned Innocent Praying for the Guilty: Luke 23:34

    A Prayer of Love

REFERENCES 39

    Bibles

    Books

    Internet

About the Author 41

INTRODUCTION
PRISONS AND PRAYERS
© 2019 Brenda Simuel Jackson

A space of holding is a prison while guards and uncertainty are the environmental atmosphere.

Prisons are not places of peace, but of boredom that can ring loudly. Prisons can be a locale in which to await the punishment of deeds done.

Imprisonment can be a place of injustice, but it does not block the Savior's love.

We cry from our prisons knowing that we will be heard. We cry from our prisons while seeking the freedom through His Word.

What are Biblical prisons?

The Old Testament legal system did not formally include prisons, as the legal system did not use imprisonment as a penalty for law breaking (Richards, 817). Prison was a room or place used to hold persons awaiting trial or execution (Ibid). Guards were the prisons for some where persons were held in custody under guard (Leviticus 24:12; Numbers 15:34). "Cities of refuge" were a form of prison. They were places of confinement; the place was a city. Such cities served to preserve the life of one who had accidentally killed another. There was no intent to kill. This saved the person from blood revenge. Such cities also were as places of custody until it was determined if the person killed with or without intent.

Most common prisons were natural pits or caverns in mountainous areas. Some prisons were cave-like dungeons (Youngblood, et. Al

Introduction

1031). Scriptures describe the harsh treatment persons placed in prison received (1 Kings 22:27). Persons imprisoned in pits or cisterns were expected to die there. The pits concealed the bodies (Ibid).

Persons who were prisoners of Kings or of Pharaohs were placed in a facility that was maintained for such persons (Genesis 39:20). Ordinary criminals were sent to forced labor (Richards, 818). Political or religious leaders were held as prisoners in rooms set aside in the administrative buildings (Jeremiah 32:2, 1 Kings 22:26, 27).

Youngblood (1031) describes less common prisons. These were like the prison in Gaza where Samson was bound and held (Judges 16:21, 25). Jeremiah was confined in the house of the secretary, which was converted into a prison (Jeremiah 37:15, 16). Later he was confined to an empty, muddy cistern (Jeremiah 38:6-10).

The prisons in the New Testament were similar to those in the Old Testament. There were prisons that were made from natural caves, and therefore had inner parts. The prisons in Greece and Rome were for persons awaiting trial such as Paul in Rome. Prisons were also a part of government headquarters such as the Praetorium (Palace) at Jerusalem (Mark 15:16), and the prison in Herod's judgment hall where Paul was detained (Acts 23:35; 24:27).

Be reminded, Christ voiced concern for those in prison (Matthew 5:25; 18:30-34, 25:36).

What Prayer Is

Generally, prayer is communicating with God. The NIV and the NASB encyclopedia define the Hebrew word, prayer, "a cry to one who is able to act to meet the need of the one praying" (Richards, 497). In prayer, one asks God to assess a need and to meet that need. Another definition is "an appeal for a divine decision," (Ibid).

Prayers from Prison: A Biblical Study of Faith in Captivity

The Scriptures' term for prayer is translated or interpreted as intercession (Isaiah 53:12; Jeremiah 27:18).

Relationship is a key to the process of prayer in the Old Testament. Prayer expresses a personal relationship. This relationship was initiated by God, and God is recognized as Creator and Redeemer (Richards, 497-8). Prayer is an essential part of the relationship. "...true prayer is always a matter of the heart" as demonstrated in Jeremiah 29:12-14 (Richards, 498). The character of the one praying is one of dependence and humility. The person recognizes his dependence on the One to Whom he is praying. (Ibid)

The Godhead and Prayer is Key to the Prayer Process:
Prayers are addressed to the Father. Our prayers express our trust in and submission to God. The Revell Dictionary describes four aspects in the Old Testament for a person to pray:

1. Acknowledgment of God's existence.
2. Hope that God knows and cares about us.
3. Expectation that God is able and willing to respond to us.
4. Praying as a covenant relationship with God." (810)

First John 5:14 gives reassurance that God hears a believer's prayer; God will answer our prayers according to His plan, not ours. In praying to the Father, we not only acknowledge and give Him praise as the most Holy consecrated in Heaven (Matthew 6:9), but we recognize our dependence for material and spiritual sustenance (Matthew 6:10-11). It is known that only the Father can forgive sins, and we seek such in our prayers (6:12). We seek God's guidance and leadership (6:13).

Jesus is the avenue through which our prayers are heard by God. Prayer is offered in the name of Jesus. Why? Jesus said, "I am the way, and the truth, and the life. No one comes to the Father except through me. If you really knew me you would know my Father as

Introduction

well" (John 14:6-7a). Praying in Christ's name says we accept Jesus' rescue (salvation) through His crucifixion on the cross. We identify with Jesus and His character (Revell, 810). Praying in the name of Jesus is an indication of being in harmony with Him. "...sinners who have not trusted Jesus Christ for their salvation remain separated from God. Unbelievers may pray, but lacking fellowship, their prayers are not effective." We should only ask those in relationship with God to pray for us.

The Holy Spirit is a participant in true prayer with the Father. "...the Spirit helps us in our weakness. We do not know what we ought to pray for, but the Spirit Himself intercedes for us with groans that words cannot express. And He who searches our hearts knows the mind of the Spirit, because the Spirit intercedes for the saints in accordance with God's will." (Romans 8:26-27)

There are six basic reasons we pray:

1. To confess
2. To intercede
3. To praise God
4. To make supplication
5. To give thanks
6. To worship our God.

This writing is an analysis of prayers in the Scriptures of persons imprisoned at the time of their conversations with God. These prayers are extracted from the Old and the New Testaments. Incarceration is not a block to having effective communication with God. Incarceration does not block one's trust and confidence in our sovereign Lord.

In conclusion remember the words of the song, "The Beautiful Garden of Prayer" by Eleanor Allen Schroll, 1920:

> "There's a garden where Jesus is waiting, There's a place that is wondrously fair, For it glows with the

light of His presence – 'Tis the beautiful garden of prayer.

O the beautiful garden of prayer, O the beautiful garden of prayer! There my Savior awaits, and He opens the gates to the beautiful garden of prayer."

Prisoner #1
Sampson – Judges 16:28-30

Then Samson prayed to the Lord, "Sovereign Lord, remember me. O God, please strengthen me just once more, and let me with one blow get revenge on the Philistines for my two eyes....Samson said, 'Let me die with the Philistines.'"

The life and death of Samson are recorded in Judges 13:1-16:31. Samson was born and raised as a Nazerite (a person specially dedicated to God). God has assigned Samson to begin the deliverance of Israel from the hand of the Philistines. The Philistines dominated, although the Israelites had intermingled with the Philistines (Revell, 888). Samson battled the Philistines and through the power of the Holy Spirit, he won victory after victory (Judges 15:13-17). Samson's life had three dominant themes:

1. The Spirit of God was active in Samson. His physical strength was from the Spirit of God (Judges 13:25; 14:6, 19; 15:14).
2. Samson's strength enabled him to perform spectacular feats.
3. Samson was morally weak which caused his downfall. His weakness caused him to violate his position of being set aside for God's purpose. He violated the Nazerite vows: A Nazerite was not to cut his hair (Judges 14:8, 9, 10; 16:19), and he married a Philistine, just to name two.

Samson allowed his flesh to dominate him. This led to his defeat, and his being imprisoned, losing his eyesight, and giving the Philistines the opportunity to honor their false god, Dagon, the god of grain (Judges 16:23-24).

There are many who are imprisoned because they gave in to the flesh, and they went after material gains; they shut Jesus and the

Holy Spirit out of their lives. Many are angry at the "system", and some seek to retaliate because of their incarceration.

Samson was his own enemy, but he maintained his belief in a sovereign God, and he prayed.

Samson's prayer for victory included a request for deliverance. The answer for this request was suicide. Samson' prayer was a petition for revenge. He was willing to die to get revenge for his lost sight. Samson's prayer lined up with God's purpose for him, to start the deliverance of Israelite from the Philistines. Samson killed more Philistines when he died than while he lived. It was Samson's job to destroy the enemy, not to love them (Wiersbe, 155). God answered Samson's prayer. This may suggest that he was back in God's will (Psalm 66:18-20). Samson's life lets us know that when we have sinned, we should call on the Lord, as did David (read Psalm 32).

Sin and Prayer
© 2019 Brenda Simuel Jackson

I know when I have sinned through disobeying
God's Will and His Word.

My prayer is not be one of excuse of how
I simply followed the way of the world.

My prayer is not to try and cover-up my sin.
My prayer is not to try and blame Satan.

My prayer is to confess my wrong against my sovereign God,
and to seek His forgiveness.

My prayer is to repent and turn my focus and my life back to my
Creator and Father asking for His deliverance.

Prisoner #2
Jeremiah's Conversation with God: Jeremiah 6:10

Jeremiah laments:

"To whom can I speak and give warning? Who will listen to me? Their ears are closed so they cannot hear. The word of the Lord is offensive to them; they find no pleasure in it.

The Lord replies in vv11-30.

Jeremiah's prophetic ministry began in 626 BC and ended in or after 586 BC. Jeremiah was a priest, a member of the household of Hilkiah. His hometown was anathorth (1:1). Jeremiah is seen as a prophet of doom. The Lord commanded him not to marry and raise children because of future divine judgment on Judah (Introduction to the Book of Jeremiah, NIV, 1985, 1115). This judgment will annihilate the next generation (16:1-4). Jeremiah was labeled a traitor because of his theme of judgment, his counsel of submission to Babylon, and his message of life as usual for exiles of early deportation. Jeremiah was imprisoned by the Israelites. Their refusal to accept Jeremiah's message was the cause of his being imprisoned. Jeremiah's first imprisonment was in a vaulted cell, a dungeon in the house of Jonathon. Later his imprisonment was in the courtyard of the guard (37:14-16, 21). At the time of this prayer, he was imprisoned in Jerusalem (6:10).

Prayers of lament express "deep trust in Yahweh"; they help one express issues of struggling or suffering to God. Jeremiah's prayer laments a critical time when no one was listening. He tells the Lord of his concern of the condition of their hearts and ears, which were blocking out God's Word (Wiersbe, 85). The Lord answered Jeremiah's wrath by describing His wrath (6:11-30).

Prayers from Prison: A Biblical Study of Faith in Captivity

Like Jeremiah we should express our concerns, our distresses, and our anger to God. The event of being locked up should cause one to cry out. Read Psalm 88 aloud. Hear the issues of distress cried out before the Throne of Grace. Don't be afraid to cry out to the Lord.

HELP
© 2019 Brenda Simuel Jackson

Help, a cry in times of my distress
when I am overwhelmed,
even though I am doing my best.

Help me through the mess I made
and other situations also.

Lord please remove the sufferings;
Lord make them let me go.

In You, and You alone, I place my trust.
Increase my faith to know You are with me,
I am not alone, and I will not spiritually bust.

Prisoner #3
Jonah, A prophet in a living prison: Jonah 2:2-9

He said: *"In my distress I called to the Lord, and He answered me. From the depths of the grave I called for help, and You listened to my cry. You hurled me into the deep, into the very heart of the seas, and the currents swirled about me; all your waves and breakers swept over me. 'I said, I have been banished from Your sight; yet I will look again toward your holy temple.' The engulfing waters threatened me, the deep surrounded me; seaweed was wrapped around my head. To the roots of the mountains I sank down; the earth beneath barred me in forever. But You brought my life up from the pit, O Lord my God. When my life was ebbing away, I remembered You, Lord, and my prayer rose to You, to Your Holy Temple. Those who cling to worthless idols forfeit the grace that could be theirs. But I, with a song of thanksgiving will sacrifice to You. What I have vowed I will l make good. Salvation comes from the Lord."*

The name Jonah means dove. The dove has been used in the Old Testament as symbolic of one being taken advantage of or one being deceived, or as one enriched by God. In Hosea 7:11, the Prophet writes, *"Ephraim is like a dove, easily deceived and senseless."* In Psalm 68:11-13 NRSV, the Lord announced the word, *"and great was the company.... Even while you sleep among the sheepfolds, the wings of my dove are sheathed with silver, its feathers with shining gold."*

Psalm 74:19 is a plea to God for Israel, who is represented as a dove. *"Do not hand over the life of your dove to wild beasts;...."* The dove, as a simile or metaphor, gives us a glimpse of Jonah's experiences, and relates to his prayer in Jonah 2:1-9. Jonah is a real person and is referenced in 2 Kings 14:25, as a Jewish prophet from Gath Hepher in Zebulum who ministered in the Northern Kingdom of Israel. Jesus teaches about the sign of Jonah. *"For as Jonah was three days and three nights in the belly of a huge fish, so the Son of Man will be three days and three nights in the heart of the earth."* Jesus presents Jonah, is experience as a type of His own death, burial, and resurrection. Jesus references Jonah as a preacher who preached to Nineveh, who then repented (Matthew 12:40-41).

Jonah ministered from 800-750 BC. The northern Kingdom was restored by King Jeroboam II (793-753), but Assyria remained a threat to Israel. Nineveh was the capitol of Assyria, and Jonah was angry over the wickedness and persecution Israel had received from Assyria. Assyria was God's disciplinarian of Israel's disobedience. Yet God commissioned Jonah to carry a message of salvation to Nineveh. Jonah ran away and went to Joppa. Jonah's disobedience resulted in God's punishment; he was sacrificed to the sea by sailors who were caught in the middle of Jonah's saga. Jonah was swallowed by a big fish, which was his holding cell for three days (Jonah 1:1-17).

Jonah's prayer is one of thanksgiving for deliverance from death in the sea. In accordance with Jonah 2:1, Jonah prayed from inside the fish. This is the only prison, which was a living organism, although in the New Testament, a prison may have been being shackled to a guard.

The Scripture appears to relate how Jonah recalled his prayer for help as he was sinking into the sea (2:2-3). Jonah refers to his prison as a pit (2:6c). Jonah's prayer exhibited his faith in God, as he attempted to look toward God's Holy Temple (2:4,7). Jonah recounts that he remembered the Lord, and he prayed to the God he remembered (Wiersbe, 381).

Jonah is in his grave, pit, and near death. Jonah recognizes that the sailors were agents of God's judgment (2:3). Jonah's prayer includes hopeful expectation (2:4). Jonah yields to the Lord, and closes his prayer with a solemn vow (2:8,9).

Prisoner #3 - Jonah

Being in prison does not mean God will not hear you. The circumstances of despair, may prompt you to take responsibility for your actions. The greater the despair, the greater could be the deliverance (2:5). One's greatest needs may be realized in prison. We must always remember salvation; rescue is from the Lord.

"And the Lord commanded the fish, and it vomited Jonah onto dry land." (2:10)

My Personal Prison
© 2019 Brenda Simuel Jackson

A living prison I made when I ran from my Lord's command.

A living prison I made when I disobeyed, refusing His demand.

My prison was with me day and night, no matter how I tried to find the light.

I finally realized I put the chains on my life.

Unlocking the chains and bringing back my sight was committing to my Lord's direction,
and correction.

New Testament Prisoners

Prisoner #4

Rich man, a sinner sentenced to eternal imprisonment:

Luke 16:22-24; 26-28

This prayer is part of a parable of Jesus using the parable to teach his disciples (more than the twelve). It is optional to the reader to accept this prayer as a genuine petition, a prayer of intercession, and not simply an illustration.

"The time came when the beggar died and the angels carried him to Abraham's side. The rich man also died and was buried. In Hades, where he was in torment, he looked up and saw Abraham far away, with Lazarus by his side. So he called to him, 'Father Abraham, have pity on me and send Lazarus to dip the tip of his finger in water and cool my tongue, because I am in agony in this fire.' "But Abraham replied, 'Son, remember that in your lifetime you received your good things, while Lazarus received bad things, but now he is comforted here and you are in agony. And besides all this, between us and you a great chasm has been set in place, so that those who want to go from here to you cannot, nor can anyone cross over from there to us.' "He answered, 'Then I beg you, father, send Lazarus to my family, for I have five brothers. Let him warn them, so that they will not also come to this place of torment.'

The place of the rich man is described as a confinement. He cannot leave. This is the same as a prison or jail. The commentator, Warren W. Wierse states that hell is a permanent prison of the damned before the final judgment. The damned are in a temporary prison (p. 241), we call this jail. The torment of the damned includes torment that characterizes hell. Revelation 20:10-15, describes hell and hades as a place of torment. Luke describes it as not only physical torment, but physical separation from all that is righteous.

The Talmud mentions 'Abraham's side as the name of the place of righteousness. (Lewis Foster, contributor to the NIV Study Bible, 1985, p. 1572).

The rich man in Hades begins to pray, first for himself, seeking comfort and mercy at someone else's expense. When his prayer for himself could not be answered, the rich man prays for his brothers, who like him had not accepted Jesus Christ as God, the Son. It is noted that although in torment, the rich man had not changed. He remained selfish and self-centered. He did not seek forgiveness for his treatment of Lazarus. You may describe his prayer as an arrogant argument with God. He did not demonstrate any humility. The prayer demonstrates that if in life one was closed to the witness of Christ, there are no changes in death. Those who are lost and die, remain lost, and praying for them is useless. Prayers from those in hades are useless. The time to pray is while they have the breath of life in them.

Prisoner #4 – A Rich Man

Prayer and Repentance
© 2019 Brenda Simuel Jackson

A prayer of repentance is a commitment to change.

A prayer to turn from the way of the world is the aim.

A prayer in prison for a change is a prayer for a heart of flesh and a renewed Spirit.

Such prayers are heard by God when one is living.

God hears the cries and petitions of those who are dying.

The prayers of the dead are void, not heard, and are of no impact.

Pray while you have the time not to be rejected.

Prisoner #5

The Prayers of Apostle Paul during His Imprisonments

The prayers from prison in the New Testament are prayers of Apostle Paul. As a beginning, let us review the life of Paul as a prisoner. Paul was imprisoned on four occasions, the primary cause of which was his spreading the gospel to the Gentiles. He wrote four epistles while in prison: Ephesians, Philippians, Colossians, and Philemon. Paul was imprisoned in Philippi. His companion, Silas was imprisoned with him. Although imprisoned, they planted a strong church. Paul completed two years of incarceration in the Roman Governor's headquarters in Caesarea. Following this incarceration, he was a prisoner on a ship on the way to Rome. The ship was shipwrecked. Paul spent another two years in Rome under house arrest while he was waiting for his case to come to a hearing. During the house arrest, Paul was shackled to one of the soldiers who guarded him in 4-hour shifts (Youngblood, p 954). This was the ancient form of being tethered. Paul was free to receive visitors and to talk with them. Paul was released, but then arrested and held in prison in Rome where he was martyred.

Prayer from a Dungeon: Acts 16:25-34

About midnight Paul and Silas were praying and singing hymns to God, and the other prisoners were listening to them. Suddenly there was such a violent earthquake that the foundations of the prison were shaken. At once all the prison doors flew open, and everyone's chains came loose.... The jailer called for lights, rushed in and fell trembling before Paul and Silas. He then brought them out and asked, "Sirs, what must I do to be saved?" They replied, "Believe in the Lord Jesus, and you will be saved – you and your household."

The prayers of Paul and Silas were in direct contrast to their physical situation. Paul and Silas were physically bound, their feet in stocks (Acts 16:24). The jail was a cavern-like cell, built into a natural cave. The hearts of Paul and Silas were free. They were spiritually free, which gave them joy to pray and to give praises to God. Prior to being thrown in prison, Paul and Silas were severely flogged. Their physical treatment did not stop their joy in the Lord (v25). The Lord responded having received the prayers and praises. Supernatural deliverance occurred: an earthquake, a shaking of the prison, an opening of locked doors, the falling off of chains, and the inmates who did not flee (v26). Why did Paul stay? He was an Apostle to the Gentiles. The jailer was a Gentile. He was about to kill himself. "If a prisoner escaped, the life of the guard was demanded in his place. To commit suicide would shorten shame and distress (NIV Study Bible comments, 1678)." The jailer seeing the events asked, "What must I do to be saved (v30)?" The jailer seeking salvation and Paul's response is the essence of the Great Commission (Matthew 28:16-20).

Physical imprisonment does not incarcerate one spiritually or stop one's relationship with the Godhead. Paul's and Silas' joy was seen and heard by other prisoners. Although incarcerated, one's spiritual light can shine, provide encouragement to others, and open opportunities for others to recognize that they can be set free.

Free in a Cage
© 2012 Brenda Simuel Jackson

Locked in a cage, but I'm free as I can be through the Holy Spirit Who lives in me.

Having the mind of Christ helps me stay focused on the positive aspects of my life.

Prisoner #5 – The Apostle Paul

Although the C/O tells me when I can get up in the morning, the HOLY Spirit gives me peace enabling me to see each day dawning.

During the shake down, my small space was no longer my own, but the kindness through the Holy Spirit allowed humility to remind me, the space was only on loan.

I had signed up for the seminar, but my name was not on the call-out list. The self-control in me produced a calmness and not a fist. I can interact freely with inmates, the Chaplain, and COs because my faith directs my tone and communication as I go.

My body is locked in a cage, but the Spirit in me controls my mind, emotions, and actions giving me freedom in every aspect of the way.

I learned that how I wait is a choice given to me, and when I don't quench the Spirit's power, my choices set me free.

Locked in a cage? I am free through the love of the One who gave His life for me, giving me a freedom from above and in eternity.

Pauline Epistle in Prison: Ephesians 1:15-20

For this reason, ever since I heard about your faith in the Lord Jesus and your love for all the saints, I have not stopped giving thanks for you, remembering you in my prayers. I keep asking that the God of our Lord Jesus Christ, the glorious Father, may give you the Spirit of wisdom and revelation, so that you may know Him better. I pray also that the eyes of your heart may be enlightened in order that you may know the hope to which he has called you, the riches of His glorious inheritance in the saints, and His incomparably great power for us who believe. That power is like the working of His mighty strength, which He exerted in Christ when He raised Him from the dead and seated Him at His right hand in the heavenly realm,...

Prayers from Prison: A Biblical Study of Faith in Captivity

The epistle of Ephesians places emphasis on the unity of the church as the body of Christ. Paul expresses praise for unity and praise for the blessing shared by all believers in Christ (Gundry, 397). The prayer is a petition for perception and power. Paul starts the prayer with thanksgiving for the Ephesians accepting Christ as their Savior, and because of their faithfulness. Paul prays that the Ephesians will receive "the Spirit of wisdom" (v 17). Paul was in Ephesus a few years, and his prayer is from a prison in Rome (NIV Bible Commentary, 1789).

Paul's prayer of thanksgiving was given only when the Ephesians came to faith. He therefore had knowledge of how they were progressing in the faith. In verse 17, we find Paul praying for spiritual growth as he prays that the Ephesians would have spiritual insight. "Eyes of your heart may be enlightened," vv 18-19, refers to spiritual understanding, a picture of the heart seeing with eyes of divine illumination, understanding (Radmacher, 1533). His prayer stresses true hope. In Him we find true hope and true riches. What is hope? It is assurance of eternal life, which has been guaranteed by the gift of the Holy Spirit (v 18).

Paul's prayer places emphasis that all believers have an inheritance from God and belong to Him. Paul extols on how the Holy Spirit, Who raised Jesus (v20) is the same Spirit at work in believers (v19).

The believer is reminded that Jesus, The Christ, is in the highest place of authority at the right hand of God (v 20). This prayer of thanksgiving refers to the end times, the age to come (v 21).

It is important that we who are believers, give thanksgiving to God for those who have come to faith and have accepted the Gospel of Jesus Christ. It is important that we pray for their continuing spiritual growth, and unity in the body of Christ. This is a prayer not bound by location, but by your love for the saints.

Prisoner #5 – The Apostle Paul

Thanksgiving
© 2019 Brenda Simuel Jackson

Thank you, Lord, for calling family, friends, and others to yourself.

Thank you, Lord, that those who have said yes to Christ are growing with spiritual depth.

The hope in us is the expectation of sharing eternity with you.

The hope that we are strengthened while in this world to remain to our faith, true.

A Prayer for The Ephesians: Ephesians 3:14-21

For this reason, I kneel before the Father, from whom his whole family in heaven and on earth derives its name. I pray that out of His glorious riches He may strengthen you with power through His Spirit in your inner being, so that Christ may dwell in your hearts through faith. And I pray that you, being rooted and established in love, may have power, together with all the saints, to grasp how wide and long and high and deep is the love of Christ, and to know this love that surpasses knowledge – that you may be filled to the measure of all the fullness of God. Now to Him who is able to do immeasurably more than all we ask or imagine, according to His power that is at work within us, to him be glory in the church and in Christ Jesus throughout all generations, for ever and ever. Amen.

This prayer is in two parts, the prayer and the doxology which is a praise to God. Paul's prayer is directed to a sovereign God. God, the Father, who believers can know intimately through His names such as Eloheim, might, great almighty, (Gen. 17:1; 35:11; Isaiah 9:6,7) Jehovah, Lord which is often used with Eloheim (Gen. 28:13 meaning to be or being [Stone, p20]), and El-Shaddai, meaning almighty in supplying needs. With this intimacy in mind, Paul looks back to the reconciliation of Jews and Gentiles in Christ, read Ephesians 2:1-22.

The prayer contains two basic requests: strength (Eph. 3:16-17) and knowledge (vv18-19). Paul continues his thoughts in prayer as seen in 3:14, "sake of Gentiles, I kneel". This expresses deep emotions and reverence to God. Paul is praying to God for family. "The concept family is birth from 'being', coming from the Father, God. God is our Father, and we pray to and commit our prayers to Him. Ephesians 3:17 indicates believers in prayer are at home because Christ is already present in the believer (Romans 8:9). This prayer grows out of Paul's awareness that God is acting in believers, and God has given the believer power and love (vv 3:14-21).

The believer's knowledge of God's love is personal and intellectual. God's love is individual and corporate. Rydelnik writes that the goal of this knowledge is growing to be all that God wants us, believers to be (p. 1851). This prayer, which concerns knowledge is an in-depth way of referring to Christ's love for believers, Gentile and Jew. We are indwelled with the Holy Spirit, at the time of faith and confession. We also have spiritual power through the indwelling of Christ. Christ is at home in us through faith in Him (vv 3:16-19).

A request for strength: The inner being is parallel to the heart, emotions an will when referring to self (Romans 7:22; 2 Cor. 4:16). God has sufficient resources, and is able to meet our needs. Ephesians 3:19 lets us know we cannot fully know God's power, but God is infinite in all His attributes, and we draw on His resources and His love. In vv 20-21, the closing doxology, it encourages readers to praise God. The reader is reminded of His power and requested to give Him glory. Giving God glory is the goal of our existence as the body of Christ.

Imprisonment does not stop the power, the love of God for the believer nor the love in the believer for other believers and for the glory of God. We must maintain our intimacy, regardless of location, and remember the character of God.

The Bond that Binds Family
© 2019 Brenda Simuel Jackson

Love that maintains family ties cannot be broken.

Our Heavenly Father is Love.

We are His family.

Our love is our obedience to Him.

Our love is our concern for each other.

Love makes us one body in Christ.

We are unity with one another.

Paul's Prayer for Philippians: Philippians 1:1-11

Paul and Timothy, servants of Christ Jesus, To all God's holy people in Christ Jesus at Philippi, together with the overseers and deacons: Grace and peace to you from God our Father and the Lord Jesus Christ. I thank my God every time I remember you. In all my prayers for all of you, I always pray with joy because of your partnership in the gospel from the first day until now, being confident of this, that he who began a good work in you will carry it on to completion until the day of Christ Jesus. It is right for me to feel this way about all of you, since I have you in my heart and, whether I am in chains or defending and confirming the gospel, all of you share in God's grace with me. God can testify how I long for all of you with the affection of Christ Jesus.

And this is my prayer: that your love may abound more and more in knowledge and depth of insight, so that you may be able to discern what is best and may be pure and blameless for the day of Christ, filled with the fruit of righteousness that comes through Jesus Christ–to the glory and praise of God.

Paul opens this prayer with a Christian tone of grace and peace (v2). [Greek language], "gift" is a noun, "a reason to rejoice" as a verb, being in harmony, verb, to be, is being at peace, set an appropriate atmosphere for Paul although he is in prison, probably in Rome. Our circumstances should not prohibit positive prayers for others. Paul's joyful thanksgiving is for the readers' response to the good news of the gospel. Paul's theme is joy (Radmacher, et al, 1545). Paul is thankful that the Philippians partner with him by the active support of his ministry. They supported not only in receiving the word but through financial support (v 4:15).

The first day (1:5) of Paul's visit to Philippi (Acts 16:12) to the time of writing the letter is toward the end of Paul's first imprisonment in Rome (Acts 28:16-31). His prayer is one of confidence and joy that God has forgiven them for their sins and for the righteousness (Philippians 1:11), that is in them (Radmacher, 1545). The term work is in reference to God's activity in saving the readers/hearers.

The "day of Christ's return" is when salvation will be brought to completion. God is the initiator of salvation. God continues the process of salvation, and God is the One who will consummate the process. Imprisonment cannot block sharing in God's grace (v7). Paul has such a deep compassionate love which reaches out without partiality and without exception. This is Paul's legacy from the compassionate love exhibited by Jesus Christ. Paul in prison is anxious about the well-being of the Philippians rather than the Philippians being anxious for Paul.

Paul's theme for prayer in verses 9-11 are love, growth, wisdom, knowledge, and good works (Rydelnik, 1858). Paul prays the believer will have wise love, with the ability for improved discernment (Ibid). Real love requires growth. Love grows through knowledge (v9).

Christian love is not sentimental; it is rooted in knowledge and understanding. The focus of knowledge is God (Radmacher, 1546). Paul prayed for the highest form of Christ's love, based on unconditional commitment (Ibid). Discernment (v10) is to know what is morally and ethically superior. The goal of Christian living is to be without any mixture of evil and not being open to censure because of moral or spiritual failure. So that you may approve (discern in NIV) what is best...pure...blameless (v10). The purpose of increasing in love, which is controlled by knowledge is to be able to evaluate people and situations wisely.

Paul's prayer describes wise love enabling one to make excellent choices to produce a sincere and blameless life (Rydelnik, 1859). The result of growing in love is that God will be honored and pleased (v11). Righteousness has fruit which is shown in one's behavior (Ibid, 1547). The fruit is produced by Christ in union with Him through the work of the Holy Spirit. Philippians 1:11 is the ultimate goal of all that God does in believers.

Prisoner's Love
© 2019 Brenda Simuel Jackson

Bars cannot stop my love for those physically free.

Imprisonment does not take praise and joy from me.

I can boldly pray that my knowledge of God through Jesus Christ will continue to grow.

Those on the outside, will also know that prison does not stop one from proper behavior showing.

Although separated in space, believers are together through the Holy Spirit and God's grace.

Paul's fervent prayers for believers in Christ should be a guide to all believers.

Nothing should stop a believer from interceding for the well-being and growth of others.

Knowing God's Will: Colossians 1:9-14

For this reason, since the day we heard about you, we have not stopped praying for you and asking God to fill you with the knowledge of His will through all spiritual wisdom and understanding. And we pray this in order that you may live a life worthy of the Lord and may please Him in every way: bearing fruit in every good work, growing in the knowledge of God, being strengthened with all power according to His glorious might so that you may have great endurance and patience, and joyfully giving thanks to the Father, who has qualified you to share in the inheritance of the saints in the kingdom of light. For He has rescued us from the dominion of darkness and brought us into the Kingdom of the Son He loves, in whom we have redemption, the forgiveness of sin.

Paul's prayer of intercession is a petition to God to give the Colossian Christians, who are new in the faith, in knowledge, in wisdom, in strength, and in joy (Ramacher, 1561). Paul prayed that these new believers would grow into Christian maturity. He prayed that such growth would have good fruit. They could walk before God, please God through their good work (Ibid).

Paul prayed that the Colossians would obtain full knowledge of God's will. With such knowledge, there is wisdom and spiritual understanding. Wisdom is the practical application of knowledge

(James 3:17). Knowledge of God's will cannot be separated from spiritual understanding that comes through discernment by the Holy Spirit (Ibid). A lifestyle worthy of the gospel has three components: knowledge, wisdom, and understanding (Col. 1:9-10). Walking worthy of the Lord reflects what God has done for the Colossians (1:10). All Colossians are empowered with God's power. The Colossians were combating false teachers (NIV Study Bible, p. 1811). Paul prays they will have patience longsuffering regardless of injury, and insult and they will have joy (1:11).

Paul prays that the Colossians are qualified by God. It is God Who makes them sufficient in Christ (1:12). Where is the Kingdom of light? Paul's prayer gives the answer. The blessing of sharing eternal life, is the believer's inheritance in God's Kingdom which is heaven (Rydelnik 1869). Light is symbolic of holiness, truth, love, and life which is the result of knowing and applying God's Will.

Not My Will But Your Will
© 2019 Brenda Simuel Jackson

My morning prayers include, "Father help me to know and to do Your will today."

To know His will, I must turn to His Word to learn the Way.

It seems that each day there are obstacles trying to block my path.

I have to stop, take a breath, and pray, "Lord, please help me to know what trial I have,

help me to see that it is Your will and not mine,

and that I, through the strength of Jesus, will be patient and able to follow Your line."

Imprisonment did not stop Paul from seeking to do God's will, and it should not stop any believer, even though incarcerated.

Prisoner #6
The Imprisoned Innocent Praying for the Guilty: Luke 23:34

Father, forgive them, for they do not know what they are doing.

Jesus, the innocent is being executed on the cross. Jesus had just entered the city in triumph at the beginning of the week (19:28-38). Four days later, He was betrayed for 30 pieces of silver (22:1-22), and five days later Jesus was arrested and tried (22:27-71). Jesus was sentenced to die through crucifixion, and He died affixed to an upright wooden stake. He had been condemned as a criminal of the State and sentenced to a slow death of excruciating pain; sentenced to die in shame. His death followed being pierced in His head with thorns called a crown and being whipped with leather and metal nails to strip Him of His skin. His disciples had run to hide in fear, but He prayed to His Father, "Forgive them." He interceded for His killers, His enemies.

The killing of Jesus, His humanity, was intentional, there was a purpose. But trying to kill the anointed, was unintentional. Unintentional sin does not remove the guilt of sin on its own. Leviticus 4:13: *If the whole Israelite community sins unintentionally and does what is forbidden...guilty.* When anyone sins unintentionally, sacrifice must be made. We see Jesus, the Perfect Sacrifice, interceding for those for whom He is being sacrificed. Today we know that there are different levels/kinds of crimes of murder: murder with intent, murder by accident, and murder without intent. Regardless, there is still the stain of guilt. A jury determines the level of guilt. The law/judge determines the penalty to be paid. Only God can remove the stain of guilt.

David understood the situation as stated in Psalm 19:12, *Who can discern his error? Forgive my hidden faults.* Christ did not make a distinction; He interceded for all. He said, *Father forgive them for they do not know what they are doing.*

Jesus demonstrates what we should do when faced with the enemy. We should pray for our enemies; we should love our enemies through forgiveness and remove ignorance of salvation through our witness.

The prayer of intercession for forgiveness gave unmerited favor, grace. Forgive says the debt owed by transgressors has been paid, and the sins of mankind have been blotted out. The sinner has been released from the penalty of sin. This was a gift received by all from the cross.

Sins have been removed from sight (Psalm 103). Even if the one who committed wrong does not repent, we must pray for them and harbor no ill feelings.

Christ needed no forgiveness, yet He was dying on the cross. It is us who are born in sin and need forgiveness and salvation (Psalm 51). Jesus' prayer overlooked the ignorance of mankind.

John 1:10, *He was in the world, and the world was made through Him, and the world did not know Him.* The prayer of Jesus was for Jews, Romans, His killers, and future sinners.

A Prayer of Love
© 2019 Brenda Simuel Jackson

I may not like you,
but I love you and can pray for you.

Prisoner #6 – Jesus Christ

Jesus' love taught us to give love unconditionally.
I do not seek a reward for loving those
who wronged me intentionally.

My communication with my Father is undergirded by the authority
of my Savior, Jesus Christ.

Jesus Christ gave me His love when He died for me, paid my sin
debt, and gave me eternal life.

Amen

As you consider the various prayers collected here may you realize that the liberty obtained through faith in Christ, provides each of us the wonderful opportunity to be heard by our Heavenly Father, no matter what our circumstance.

Closing Prayer: 1 John 5:13-15

I write these things to you who believe in the name of the Son of God so that you may know that you have eternal life. This is the confidence we have in approaching God: that if we ask anything according to his will, he hears us. And if we know that he hears us—whatever we ask—we know that we have what we asked of him.

May the peace and joy obtained through the knowledge of our Lord cause you to rejoice in the reality that He loves you, hears your prayers, and wants to answer in ways that bring Him glory, and you – joy!

REFERENCES
Bibles

Barker, Kenneth. (General Editor). *The NIV Study Bible*, Grand Rapids: Zondervan Bible Publishers, 1985.

Thompson, Frank Charles (Compiler and Editor). *The Thompson Chain-Reference Bible, Newb American Standard*. Indianapolis: B.B. Kirkbride Bible Co., Inc. USA, 1993.

Books

Bible Exposition Commentary, Old Testament, Isaiah – Malachi. Colorado Springs: David Cook, 2002.

Fee, Gordon D. & Stuart, Douglas. *How to Read the Bible for all its Worth*. Grand Rapids: Zondervan, 2003.

Dockery, David S. (General Editor). *Holman Bible Handbook*. Nashville: Holman Bible Publishers, 1992.

Gundry, Robert H. *A Survey of the New Testament*. Grand Rapids: Zondervan, 1994.

Lockyer, Herbert. *All the Prayers of the Bible. A Devotional and Expositional Classic*. Grand Rapids: Zondervan Publishing, 1959.

New International Encyclopedia of Bible Words. Grand Rapids: Zondervan Publishing House, 1991.

Richards, PhD. Lawrence O. *The Revell Bible Dictionary*. New Jersey: Fleming H. Revell Co., 1990.

Radmacher, Earl D., Allen Ronald B., House, H Wayne. *New Illustrated Bible Commentary*. Nashville: Thomas Nelson, 1999.

Prayers from Prison: A Biblical Study of Faith in Captivity

Rydelnik, Michael & Vanlaningham, Michael. *The Moody Bible Commentary*. Chicago: Moody Publishers, 2014.

Schroll Eleanor Allen, "The Beautiful Garden of Prayer", *The New National Baptist Hymnal*. Nashville: National Baptist Publishing Board, 1977, p. 330.

Stone, Nathan. *Names of God*. Chicago: Moody Press, 1944.

Walvoord, John F. and Zuck, Roy B. *The Bible Knowledge Commentary*. Colorado Springs: Chariot Victor, 1983.

Wiersbe, Warren W. *The Bible Exposition Commentary, New Testament, Vol I Matthew – Galatians*. Colorado Springs: Cook Co., 1989.

Youngblood, Ronald F (General Editor). *Nelson's New Illustrated Bible Dictionary*. Nashville: Thomas Nelson, 1995.

Internet

"How Long Was The Apostle Paul Imprisoned?" Quora, 30 May 2019, www.quora.com/How-long-was-The-Apostle-Paul-imprisoned.

About the Author

Minister Brenda Simuel Jackson, Ph.D.

Brenda Simuel Jackson (BA, MA, Master of Divinity, Ph.D.) is a born again Christian, affiliated with the Baptist Denomination. She is a member and Minister of New Prospect Missionary Baptist Church, and does ministry through BSJ Christian Seminars, Inc., a 501(c)3 Prison/Jail Ministry. She is a graduate of Wayne State University, Moody Theological Seminary – Michigan, formerly Michigan Theological Seminary, and Jacksonville Theological Seminary.

Dr. Jackson has over thirty years of professional experience in human services, education administration, and management, as well as part-time collegiate instruction. She is currently a Spiritual Guide at The Federal Correctional Institution in Milan Michigan and adjunct faculty member of Owens Community College, Ohio.

Dr. Jackson is a published writer. Her eighth book, Prayers from Prison, was completed in 2019.

Dr. Jackson also hosted a radio broadcast, "God's Teaching Moments". Her Christian Journey includes short term outreach mission and prison ministry assignments in Japan, South Africa, Jamaica, Ghana, Zambia, Swaziland, Botswana, and Kenya.

Dr. Jackson is a called minister of the Gospel. She was ordained to Gospel ministry November 30, 2018. She was licensed as a minister of the Gospel November 13, 2005 and Ordained as a Chaplain with the International Association of Chaplains, March 31, 2010. Her vineyard is the prisons of the world.

www.ingramcontent.com/pod-product-compliance
Lightning Source LLC
Chambersburg PA
CBHW062040120526
44592CB00035B/1791